WORLD WAR II
50TH ANNIVERSARY

BATTLE OF THE ATLANTIC

by

Wallace B. Black
and
Jean F. Blashfield

CRESTWOOD HOUSE
New York

Maxwell Macmillan Canada
Toronto

Maxwell Macmillan International
New York Oxford Singapore Sydney

Library of Congress Cataloging-in-Publication Data

Black, Wallace B.
Battle of the Atlantic / by Wallace B. Black and Jean F. Blashfield. — 1st ed.
p. cm. — (World War II 50th anniversary series)
Includes index.
Summary: An account of the struggle by Allied forces to keep the North Atlantic free of German U-boats during World War II.
ISBN 0-89686-558-4
1. World War, 1939–1945 — Campaigns — Atlantic Ocean — Juvenile literature. [1. World War, 1939–1945 — Campaigns — Atlantic Ocean.] I. Blashfield, Jean F. II. Title. III. Series: Black, Wallace B. World War II 50th anniversary series.
D770.B59 1991
940.54'21 — dc20

91-7989
CIP
AC

Created and produced by B & B Publishing, Inc.

Picture Credits
National Archives - pages 8, 13, 21, 23, 25, 29, 39, 41, 44 (top), 45 (top left, center right)
Imperial War Museum - pages 4, 6, 7, 10, 12, 16, 17, 18, 20, 22, 27, 31, 35, 37, 44 (bottom), 45 (center left, bottom)
U.S. Navy - pages 3, 11, 15, 21, 34, 39, 44
EBG Graphics - pages 42-43

CRESTWOOD HOUSE

Macmillan Publishing Company
866 Third Avenue
New York, NY 10022

Maxwell Macmillan Canada, Inc.
1200 Eglinton Avenue East
Suite 200
Don Mills, Ontario M3C 3N1

Macmillan Publishing Company is part of the Maxwell Communication Group of Companies.

Printed in the United States of America

First Edition

10 9 8 7 6 5 4 3 2 1

CONTENTS

Chapter 1

BLITZKRIEG AT SEA

When World War II started in Poland on September 1, 1939, the German army used its famous blitzkrieg ("lightning war") tactics on land. At sea, the *Kriegsmarine* (German navy) also struck with lightning speed. The first phase of the Battle of the Atlantic began just two days later.

It was nine o'clock in the evening of September 3 as the British ocean liner *Athenia* sailed over calm seas. The huge ship had left England earlier that day, bound for Halifax, Canada. Many of its 1,300 passengers were fleeing the war.

Over smooth seas the brightly lit ship sailed along about 200 miles west of Ireland. Many passengers were just finishing dinner. The ship's orchestra was beginning to play for an evening of dancing and entertainment.

Suddenly a violent explosion rocked the ship! The German submarine U-30 had torpedoed the defenseless ocean liner without warning. The U-boat captain claimed that he thought the *Athenia* was an armed merchant ship. The 1,300 passengers took to the lifeboats as the ship started to sink. Some 112 people died that terrible night.

This cruel act brought cries of outrage from Great Britain and other nations. Paying no attention, Germany ordered its U-boats to attack Allied warships and merchant ships anywhere on the high seas.

The German Navy Prepares for War

Chancellor Adolf Hitler had ordered the German navy to start preparing for war as early as 1935. In violation of

Survivors from a topedoed merchant ship being rescued by a convoy escort vessel

agreements with France, Great Britain and other Allied nations, Germany started to build a giant navy. Submarines and high-speed battle cruisers called "pocket battleships," as well as two of the largest battleships in the world, were being built.

By September 1, 1939, the Germans had 17 submarines, the pocket battleship *Graf Spee* and other warships already at sea. They were ready to attack British and other Allied shipping the moment war broke out.

The main task of the German navy was to cut off supplies to Great Britain. Because it is a small island nation, Great Britain receives most of its food and other supplies from abroad. Hitler ordered German U-boats and other warships to attack Allied merchant ships or warships wherever they were found. Within just a few weeks dozens of British ships had been sunk.

Torpedoed by a German U-boat, the British liner Athenia *was sunk only two days after World War II began.*

Totally unprepared for U-boat warfare, the British aircraft carrier HMS Courageous *was sunk by German submarines.*

British Aircraft Carrier Sunk

Searching for submarines, the aircraft carrier HMS *Courageous* was operating just off the southwest coast of Ireland. On September 17, undetected, U-boat captain Commander Otto Schuhart maneuvered his undersea boat close to the giant warship. He fired his torpedoes with deadly accuracy. The carrier's steel sides collapsed, boilers burst, ammunition stores exploded and flaming oil coated the surrounding waters. Over 500 British sailors died.

This was a great blow to the British navy. Aircraft carriers and other large battleships were too valuable to lose while hunting U-boats. Not made for submarine warfare, they were replaced by destroyers, high-speed subchasers and aircraft from Royal Air Force (RAF) Coastal Command.

Large underwater and floating magnetic mines also took their toll on British merchant ships. The Germans planted hundreds of mines around British harbors. In addition, German aircraft began attacking Allied shipping that came within their range. And the high-speed surface raiders *Graf*

Spee and *Deutschland* attacked Allied shipping in the North and South Atlantic Ocean. By the end of 1939 the *Kriegsmarine* had sunk over 200 ships.

The Attack at Scapa Flow

On the evening of October 13, 1939, Lt. Commander Guenther Prien, captain of the German U-boat U-47, entered the huge harbor at Scapa Flow in northern Scotland. Dozens of British warships were anchored there. Captain Prien was able to sneak into the harbor for a night attack.

Aerial photographs had given Prien information he needed to make his attack. The channels leading into the harbor were partially blocked by sunken ships and other traps. But the U-boat successfully avoided them. It entered the harbor without being seen by any of the British defenders.

The HMS Royal Oak *was one of the most powerful battleships afloat. At Scapa Flow it was an easy target for the U-47.*

Cruising slowly, with the conning tower of the U-boat above the surface, Captain Prien searched the harbor for targets. Suddenly he spotted the dim shapes of ships dead ahead. He immediately identified his chosen target, the battleship HMS *Royal Oak*. After locating the huge ship he moved within range and fired four torpedoes. After waiting a few breathless minutes the German submariners heard only one loud explosion. Three of the torpedoes had been duds and the other appeared to have exploded harmlessly. Turning away, Prien fired another torpedo from his rear tubes. It too was a dud.

Certain that his ship would soon be discovered, Commander Prien headed his U-boat back toward the harbor entrance. But no alarm sounded. The British sailors did not suspect that a submarine had caused the explosion.

Miraculously Prien had a chance for another shot at his target. Reloading his torpedo tubes, he turned back into position to attack. The U-47 drew even closer to the *Royal Oak* and fired its torpedoes once again. This time the torpedoes found their mark. Suddenly the night was filled with violent explosions and flames. Within just a dozen minutes the *Royal Oak* rolled over and sank. Over 800 British sailors lost their lives.

Now under attack from British anti-submarine forces, the U-47 sped back to the harbor entrance. Again with great luck on his side, Commander Prien made his way through the dangerous channel and entered the open sea to escape his attackers.

Chapter 2

GERMAN RAIDERS AT LARGE

The start of World War II had caught the German navy only partially prepared for all-out war. Hitler had promised navy commanders that war would not come until 1944. As a result the battleships, aircraft carriers, submarines and other needed ships and supplies were not ready.

The commander in chief of the *Kriegsmarine*, Grand Admiral Erich Raeder, knew that he had a tough battle on his hands. So in the fall of 1939 he had to do the best he could with his submarines and his pocket battleships, the *Graf Spee* and *Deutschland.* These two heavily armed and high-speed battle cruisers were turned loose on the Atlantic Ocean where they began to sink Allied shipping.

Battle of the River Plate

The *Graf Spee* and *Deutschland* were highly acclaimed pocket battleships. They were less than one-third the weight

The light cruiser HMS Ajax *was part of the British force that attacked the German pocket battleship* Graf Spee *in the South Atlantic Ocean.*

The mighty Graf Spee *as it appeared before its dramatic ending in the River Plate*

of a full-size battleship. But these smaller, heavily armored raiders carried 11-inch guns, could cruise at a speed of 28 knots (about 32 miles per hour) and had a range of over 21,000 miles. They were designed for the specific task of destroying enemy shipping on the high seas.

The *Graf Spee* was commanded by veteran Captain Hans Langsdorff. Already at sea on September 1, the raider headed into the South Atlantic. On September 30 it made its first kill. It intercepted and sank the British merchant ship *Clement.* Within the next three weeks the *Graf Spee* sank three more ships.

Just as important as the sinking of the ships was the fact that the *Graf Spee* kept half of the British Atlantic fleet occupied looking for it.

By early December 1939 the *Graf Spee* had sunk a total of nine merchant ships. At that time Captain Langsdorff got some valuable information from papers taken from a ship the *Graf Spee* had sunk. He learned that a small group of British ships was to leave the River Plate in Uruguay in South America. The captain ordered full speed ahead and hurried to intercept them.

But on December 13 the heavy cruiser HMS *Exeter* and two light cruisers, the HMS *Ajax* and HMS *Achilles*, located the *Graf Spee.* They advanced at full speed to attack. Captain Langsdorff, disobeying orders to avoid combat with the British navy, turned to meet his attackers. He knew that the *Graf Spee* had greater firepower and speed than the British cruisers.

As the sea battle progressed, the *Exeter* was knocked out of commission by the *Graf Spee*'s big guns. But the smaller *Ajax* and *Achilles* pressed home the attack. The *Graf Spee* sought shelter in the neutral harbor of Montevideo, Uruguay, on the River Plate.

The *Graf Spee* had been hit more than 15 times and was running low on fuel and ammunition. Captain Langsdorff knew that a British force waited at the entrance to the River Plate, ready to attack if the *Graf Spee* tried to leave the harbor. Under international law, Uruguay could let the German raider stay for only 72 hours.

Certain that there was a large British force waiting for him, Captain Langsdorff transferred most of his crew to another ship. He then slowly steered the *Graf Spee* into international waters. There the remaining members of the crew abandoned the pocket battleship. A short time later those watching from shore saw and heard a gigantic flaming explosion as the *Graf Spee* blew up. Captain Langsdorff had sunk his proud ship. A few days later, after wrapping himself in his ship's battle flag, a disgraced Captain Langsdorff committed suicide.

The HMS Exeter *after being repaired following the battle with the* Graf Spee *in the South Atlantic*

Blown apart and in flames, the Graf Spee *was destroyed by its own crew to avoid battle with the British fleet.*

Chapter 3

U-BOATS AND BOMBERS

The year 1940 became a "happy time" for German U-boats. The Royal Navy was not prepared to fully protect the convoys bringing supplies to Britian. Convoys were groups of merchant ships that sailed together under the protection of naval escorts. In 1940 U-boats sank over 500 ships loaded with ammunition, food and other supplies. Luftwaffe (German air force) bombers also sank over 100 ships.

Germany only had about 50 submarines at the start of the war. Called U-boats (short for *Unterseeboot* — "undersea boat" — in German), these naval craft could travel great distances underwater. Equipped with torpedoes and deck guns, they could attack enemy vessels from on or below the surface of the water.

As the war progressed German shipyards were busy turning out bigger and better U-boats. Admiral Karl Doenitz, commander of the German U-boat fleet, believed that U-boats could win the war. At the beginning, however, Germany could only replace submarines that had been lost in combat.

Doenitz finally convinced Hitler of the importance of U-boats. Production was increased. By the end of the war over 1,000 had been built. With more U-boats available, 1940 and 1941 were years of success for German U-boats.

Submarine "Wolf Packs"

Individual submarines were able to make many successful attacks. But even though convoys were attacked again and again, most ships arrived safely in England.

An early transport version of the Focke-Wulf Condor over the coast of France. This huge bomber was used to search for Allied shipping in the Atlantic Ocean.

Admiral Doenitz then came up with the idea of using groups of submarines, called wolf packs. A group of five or more U-boats would attack a convoy all at once. As a result, the convoy escort vessels were unable to defend against every attacking U-boat.

Using radio, the first U-boat to sight a convoy would notify U-boat headquarters in France. Headquarters would notify all other undersea boats along the convoy's route. They would not attack until a wolf pack was formed.

In mid-October 1940 a British convoy of 35 ships was attacked. Five U-boats fired their torpedoes with deadly effect from around and even from within the convoy. They sank 20 Allied merchant ships. The armed escort vessels were unable to stop the U-boat wolf pack.

Bad weather and a shortage of U-boats slowed the Germans' initial success. However, they now knew that wolf pack tactics would work. In spite of improved Allied convoy defenses, Admiral Doenitz and his U-boats operated with great success.

RAF Hurricane fighters were launched by catapults from merchant ships to attack German bomber aircraft and U-boats.

Focke-Wulf Condor Bombers

The U-boats at sea received support from the air. Long-range Focke-Wulf Condor bombers acted as eyes for the submarines. The huge bombers could fly 600 miles out over the Atlantic searching for Allied shipping. Spotting a convoy, they would radio its location to U-boat headquarters. Submarines were then directed toward the convoy to attack.

In addition, the Condors, carrying full bombloads, would attack individual ships or stragglers from convoys under U-boat attack. They sank hundreds of merchant ships.

To combat the enemy in the air, anti-aircraft guns were put on escort vessels and merchant ships in convoys. RAF Hurricane fighters were placed on board some ships. They would take off from catapults (a powerful mechanism that could launch the fighter from a track mounted on the ship). The RAF fighter could then attack the Focke-Wulf Condors or surfaced submarines. After completing a mission, the fighter pilot would parachute or ditch his aircraft alongside an Allied vessel and wait to be rescued. It was a heroic and dangerous mission.

Chapter 4

THE BATTLE OF THE GIANTS

Hitler and Admiral Raeder, commander in chief of the German navy, had great hopes for their fleet of giant battle cruisers and new battleships. They thought that their high-speed and heavily armed ships could successfully destroy merchant convoys. But they ordered them to avoid direct battle with superior Royal Navy forces.

In May 1941, under the command of Vice Admiral Gunther Lutjens, the 50,000-ton battleship *Bismarck* and the heavy cruiser *Prinz Eugen* sailed to attack convoys in the North Atlantic Ocean. On May 23 the raiders were spotted by two British cruisers, HMS *Suffolk* and HMS *Norfolk*.

The mighty German battleship Bismarck *cruising at full speed in search of British naval forces*

The German ships were just west of Iceland, heading south to attack a large convoy carrying troops. The weaker British cruisers avoided battle and radioed for help. The British battleships HMS *Hood* and HMS *Prince of Wales,* on patrol several hundred miles to the southeast, received the message. The British commander ordered full speed ahead and the two battleships surged northward to intercept and attack the *Bismarck* and the *Prinz Eugen.*

Disaster for the Royal Navy

Early on the morning of May 24 the two forces came within range of each other and opened fire. The *Hood*, the largest and most powerful ship afloat, fired first. Turning into position so that both the *Hood* and *Prince of Wales* could bring their guns to bear, the *Hood* was hit. Shells from both the *Bismarck* and *Prinz Eugen* struck the huge battleship. A shell hit the *Hood*'s ammunition storerooms. Giant explosions and flames ripped through the gallant ship. Split in half, the *Hood* sank. Nearly the entire crew — over 1,400 officers and men — went down with the ship. Only three survived. The *Prince of Wales* was also damaged by shellfire and had to withdraw from the battle. It was the greatest defeat in the history of the Royal Navy.

The Bismarck *firing a broadside at HMS* Hood *in predawn darkness on May 24, 1941*

Although hit only three times, the *Bismarck* was in serious trouble. Several oil tanks were damaged and the ship was running short of fuel. But Admiral Lutjens could still gloat over his great victory. He ordered the *Prinz Eugen* to head out alone and seek another Allied convoy to attack. The *Bismarck* headed back toward a safe harbor in France for repairs.

The Royal Navy Seeks Revenge

Meanwhile, the British Home Fleet was now aware of the disaster and of the *Bismarck*'s location. The battleship *King George V,* the aircraft carrier *Victorious,* cruisers and nine destroyers entered the hunt.

Sailing through fog and rain, the captain of the *Bismarck* hoped to lose its pursuers. But the *Norfolk* and the *Suffolk* kept close on its trail. On the afternoon of May 24 the *Victorious* was close enough to launch a squadron of Fairey Swordfish torpedo planes.

The pilots flying the old, two-seat biplanes located the *Bismarck* that night and launched their torpedoes. Only one reached its target, and it failed to do any damage. However, knowing a strong force was within striking distance, Admiral Lutjens ordered the *Bismarck* to head for Saint-Nazaire in France at full speed. Due to bad weather and darkness the British lost contact with the fleeing battleship.

By this time all available resources of the Royal Navy had been called into play. Catalina PBY flying boats were searching the target area. Another aircraft carrier, HMS *Ark Royal,* was brought into the mission. Finally, on May 26 one of the Catalina flying boats sighted the ill-fated *Bismarck* and reported its position.

A second large naval group moved in from the south to cut off the *Bismarck*. The battleship HMS *Renown*, the aircraft carrier *Ark Royal* and the cruiser *Sheffield* were ready to attack. Swordfish torpedo planes, flying through bad weather, finally found their target. The Swordfish

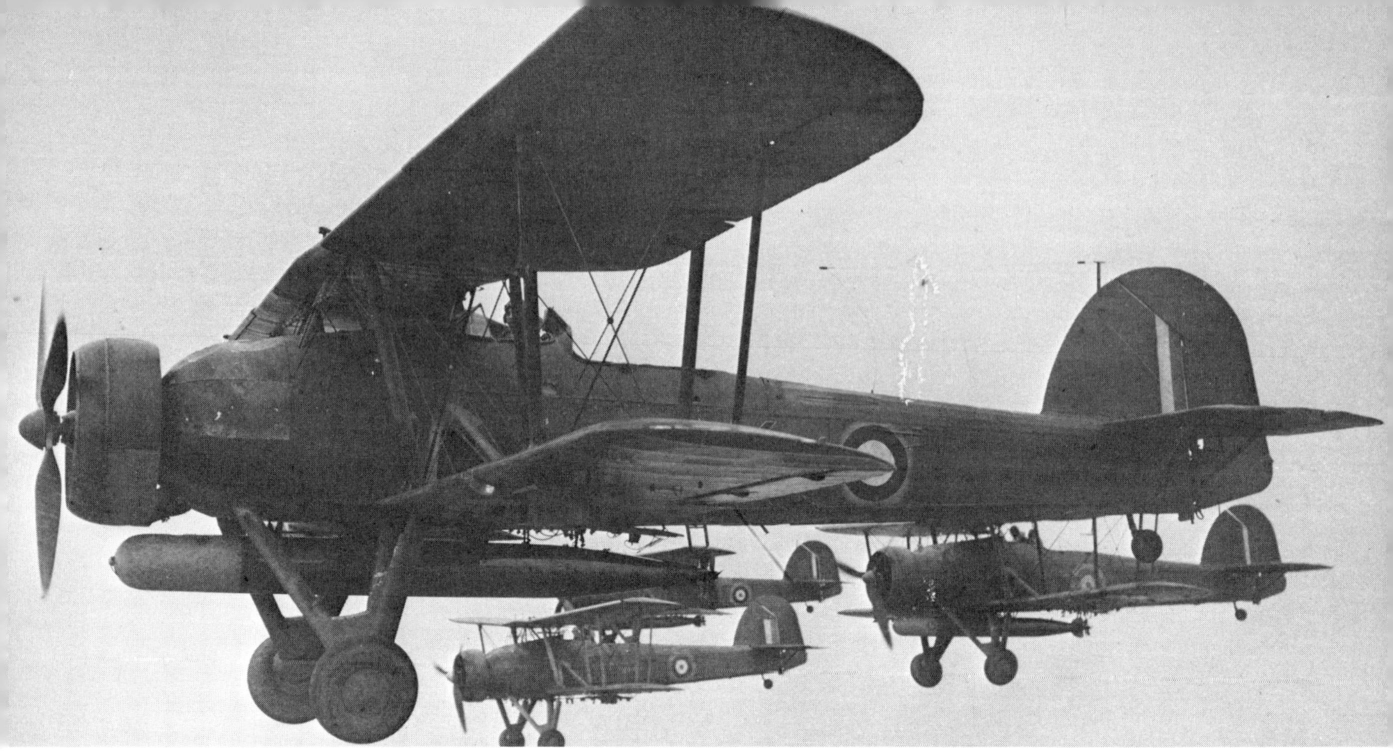

Fairey Swordfish torpedo planes successfully attacked the Bismarck *several times.*

attacked from all directions. In spite of heavy defensive fire, three torpedoes struck the *Bismarck*.

Although not mortally wounded, the *Bismarck* suffered damage to its steering gear. It was forced to slow to a speed of only eight knots and was seen turning in circles. The ship was now easy prey for the British Home Fleet. Destroyers sped to the attack and hit the doomed ship with three more torpedoes.

The next morning the battleships *King George V* and *Rodney* attacked again. Drawing close, both ships fired salvo after salvo from their big guns. The German sailors fought back bravely, but the *Bismarck*'s guns were finally silenced. As the huge battleship rolled helplessly in heavy seas, the cruiser *Dorsetshire* launched two more torpedoes into its hull. On May 27, 1941, the *Bismarck* sank. Only 100 men from its crew of over 2,200 survived.

Chapter 5

CONVOYS TO RUSSIA

In the months following the sinking of the *Bismarck,* the German battleships again tried to avoid battle. The U-boat fleet continued its successful attacks on convoys bound for England. However, now convoys were needed to deliver supplies to Russia. In June 1941 the Germans had attacked Russia. That nation was now at war on the Allied side.

All Russian Baltic and North Sea ports were blocked by the Germans. Convoys had to travel the dangerous route to the west and north of Norway and through the frigid Barents Sea to reach Russian ports. These convoys provided new targets for the German Luftwaffe, U-boats and warships based in Norway.

Russian-bound convoys were beginning to lose ships to the enemy. The German attack forces included over 200 bombers, 30 U-boats, the battleship *Tirpitz* and a dozen other cruisers and destroyers.

An Allied convoy fighting its way through stormy seas in the North Atlantic

The German battle fleet as it sails north toward Norwegian bases to combat Allied convoys bound for Russia

Through the month of May 1942, U-boats and German aircraft destroyed about 15 ships in these convoys. Many ships did get through to their destinations, but others were forced to turn back. Hundreds of merchant seamen died in the ice-filled waters off North Cape in Norway and in the Barents Sea. Each convoy lost more ships than the one before.

Slaughter in the Arctic

On June 27, 1942, the convoy called PQ-17 set sail from Iceland with 35 Allied merchant ships. They were bound for the Russian port of Archangel. Accompanying the ill-fated convoy were rescue vessels, destroyers, anti-aircraft ships, submarines, corvettes (small destroyers), minesweepers and armed trawlers. In addition, several large British and U.S. naval forces were on patrol to the south and west, ready to help. They were to fight off attacks by German surface ships.

The German high command was well informed. They knew the exact sailing date and the makeup of convoy PQ-17. Under orders from Hitler himself the German battleships *Tirpitz* and *Scheer*, the cruiser *Admiral Hipper* and seven destroyers were ready to attack the convoy. Eight U-boats were in position in the convoy's path. Over 200 German bombers were ready to strike the moment the convoy came into range.

As the Allied ships rounded the northern tip of Norway on July 3, the Germans attacked. Both U-boats and Luftwaffe bombers made successful hits through the screen of escort vessels. Several of the merchant ships were destroyed. On July 5 the battleship *Tirpitz* led a naval force from its base at Altenfjord, Norway. Fearing an attack by this strong force of surface vessels, the British convoy commander ordered the convoy to scatter. Each ship was to make its way alone toward Russia.

Without the protection of naval escorts, the individual ships were sitting ducks. One after the other, they were attacked and sunk by U-boats and Heinkel bombers of the Luftwaffe. Wreckage filled the icy seas as ships were torpedoed and bombed. Thrown into the freezing waters, many merchant seamen died from exposure in minutes. Strangely enough, the *Tirpitz* and its attack force never did make contact with the convoy and returned to their base.

Alone, or in small groups, the surviving ships sailed the last 800 miles without naval escort. By the time the last remaining ship of PQ-17 straggled into Archangel, 23 of the original 35 ships in the convoy had been lost. This disastrous event proved the importance of keeping a convoy together.

Even if German raiders were avoided, the Allied convoys had to face the ice-filled waters of the Barents Sea.

PQ-18, a 40-ship convoy, sailed in September. It stayed together with a strong naval escort. But it still lost 13 ships. These losses in Arctic convoys were severely criticized by the Russians. Their need for food and supplies blinded them to just how dangerous, costly and often thankless these missions were.

Battle of the Barents Sea

During the last half of 1942 convoys to Russia stopped. PQ-17 and PQ-18 had shown how fatal such missions could be. In addition, all ships were busy carrying troops and supplies for the invasion of North Africa.

But in December 1942, convoys to Russia started again. The northern route was still under attack by German bombers and U-boats. However, severe winter weather slowed their operations. The next convoy, JW-51A, with 15 merchant ships under heavy escort, made the trip safely.

However, the German naval commanders were ready for the next convoy, JW-51B, which also had 15 ships with a strong escort. The pocket battleship *Lützow*, the *Admiral Hipper* and an escort of six destroyers were to make the attack.

On December 30 the convoy was headed eastward about 100 miles above Norway. Late that night the German fleet left Altenfjord. The plan called for the *Hipper* to attack from north of the convoy and the *Lützow* from the south.

Heavy fog and snowstorms clouded the area. Although the attackers were in position to strike the convoy, confusing orders from German naval headquarters made them hesitate. Instead of being ordered to attack immediately, they were told to use caution and avoid contact with a heavy enemy force.

By December 31, the *Hipper* was in sight of about a dozen ships. Because of poor visibility, its commander could not tell friend from foe. Finally, after identifying several British destroyer escorts, the *Hipper* opened fire. But the cruiser itself came under attack by British destroyers.

To the south the *Lützow* had finally intercepted the convoy. But again, because of stormy skies, a German captain held off firing because he could not identify the ships.

When first attacked, the convoy commander had called a nearby Royal Navy battle group for help. At 10:30 A.M. on December 31 the British cruisers *Sheffield* and *Jamaica* along with three destroyers attacked the two German warships. Caught by surprise, the *Hipper* was immediately hit. A German destroyer was also hit by heavy fire and sank. Soon the badly commanded German force was fleeing the scene. The battle of the Barents Sea was over. Convoy JW-51B proceeded safely to its Russian destination.

Hitler, angered by the bad judgment and poor performance of the warship commanders, disbanded much of the German surface navy. It was never again a real threat to convoys bound for England or Russia. But U-boat wolf packs continued the Battle of the Atlantic with increasing success.

All merchant ships in the convoys bound for Russia carried army or navy gun crews to help fight off German aircraft.

Chapter 6

U.S. NAVY JOINS THE BATTLE

During the first years of World War II the Battle of the Atlantic seesawed back and forth. The German U-boats, bombers, surface raiders and mines were taking a terrible toll. On the other hand, the Royal Navy's giant fleet was fighting a brave defensive battle.

From September 1939 to December 1940 the British had lost more than 1,000 ships. Ships were being sunk faster than they could be built. At the same time German U-boat losses were also heavy. And the German pocket battleships had been driven from the Atlantic. However, Germany was still definitely winning the first stages of the Battle of the Atlantic.

U.S. Shipyards Go to Work

The United States had begun a naval expansion program as early as 1936. In 1940 navy shipyards began working around the clock to build a two-ocean navy to defend against a possible war with Japan and Germany. Production of merchant ships to replace British losses was increased. For the first time, ships were mass-produced. Called the Liberty Ships, the first of these famous vessels was delivered in September 1941. Over 600 new merchant ships were delivered in the next 12 months.

U.S. Neutrality Patrol

When war broke out in Europe in September 1939 the main strength of the U.S. Navy was in the Pacific. But an

Atlantic fleet was taking shape. It would include battleships, cruisers, destroyers and aircraft carriers. It would carry out a neutrality patrol of coastal waters of North and South America.

Its purpose was to see that ships of the warring nations did not fight any sea battles in neutral waters. The navy was also supposed to protect U.S. merchant ships and those of other neutral nations.

Convoys in the Atlantic

A typical convoy was made up of 50 to 60 Allied ships steaming as a group in nine to twelve columns. Individual ships and columns were separated by a thousand yards or less. Each convoy, sailing in a tightly knit square less than four miles across, was protected by a naval escort. The escort was made up of speedy, fast-turning destroyers and corvettes armed with guns, sound gear and depth charges to defend against submarines.

Always alert for attack, a giant convoy sails peacefully on smooth seas under sunny skies.

Air patrols flew over the convoys from Canada and from Great Britain for several hundred miles. Because of the limited range of patrolling bombers, there was no air cover in the middle of the Atlantic Ocean.

During the first year of the war, losses to U-boats were few. However, after the fall of Norway and France in spring 1940, Germany obtained submarine bases on the Atlantic coast of Europe. For the next two years, attacks on convoys speeded up. Sinkings occurred almost daily.

Surface raiders, German aircraft and the submarine wolf packs were sinking merchant ships and escort vessels faster than they could be replaced. The British could not exist without the supplies being brought by the battered convoys. A large part of the Royal Navy destroyer fleet had been sunk or was laid up for repairs. Great Britain needed help badly or the war would be lost.

U.S. Offers Aid

Although officially neutral, the United States sympathized with Great Britain. The neutrality patrol freed ships of the Royal Navy to protect their convoys and the British Isles. U.S. Navy patrol bombers flying neutrality-patrol missions from Canada provided air cover for departing convoys.

The U.S. Navy had a large number of old destroyers and other naval vessels left over from World War I. They had been kept in "mothballs," protected from rust and weather in case they were ever needed. They were one answer to Great Britain's many problems. Some 50 of these old "four-stackers" were turned over to the Royal Navy and put back in service. In exchange Great Britain gave the U.S. Navy the use of some of its bases in Canada, Bermuda and the Caribbean Sea.

The presence of U.S. neutrality-patrol destroyers off Canada was actually helping to defend convoys as they headed for England. German submarines were afraid to attack destroyers escorting convoys in the neutral zone for fear that they might attack a U.S. Navy ship by mistake.

U.S. Navy Defends the Western Atlantic

Even though the British lost hundreds of ships, thousands of others got through. During the course of the war the British actually lost only two percent of the ships in convoys. But early in the war, losses were much higher. To help the overworked British escort vessels, the U.S. Navy switched from patrols to active convoy escort duty.

A flying boat of the U.S. Coast Guard on neutrality patrol over the western Atlantic

During the summer of 1941, the U.S. Army and Navy set up bases in Canada, Greenland and Iceland. U.S. Navy Task Force 19 began escorting British convoys from Canada to Iceland. The Royal Navy took over from there and escorted convoys for the remainder of the voyage to the British Isles.

The first active encounter between an American naval vessel and a German U-boat took place on September 4, 1941. Along with a British patrol bomber, the destroyer USS *Greer* made contact with the U-652. The destroyer, alone and not involved in escort duty, did not attack the sub. However, after avoiding depth charges dropped by the bomber, the U-boat fired several torpedoes at the *Greer*. Fortunately they missed.

U-boats Draw First Blood

In mid-October 1941, a large convoy was cruising about 40 miles south of Iceland. Escorted by a small squadron of corvette subchasers, the convoy was attacked by a wolf pack of U-boats. Five U.S. destroyers responded to a call for help.

On October 17 the U-boats made six successful attacks on the convoy, sinking five merchant ships and damaging a destroyer, the USS *Kearny.* A British destroyer was also torpedoed and sunk. Although severely damaged and with many casualties, the *Kearny* was able to make its way to Iceland. Just two weeks later, another destroyer, the USS *Reuben James,* was also torpedoed and sunk, with the loss of 115 lives.

These two incidents ended the uneasy truce between the U.S. Navy and German U-boats. Ships of each nation were now free to attack or defend themselves when a confrontation came about. However, only one month later, on December 7, 1941, it all became official. After the Japanese attack on Pearl Harbor, the United States declared war on both Japan and Germany. And the U.S. Navy entered the Battle of the Atlantic in full force.

Sailors on an Allied destroyer drop depth charges on a German U-boat that has been located by the use of sonar.

Chapter 7

THE ALLIES FIGHT BACK

To win the Battle of the Atlantic the Allies had to develop new techniques. First of all they had to be able to find attacking U-boats. And when they found the submarines, they had to develop means of destroying them. Seamanship, courage and endurance were not enough. New technology and weapons were needed.

Sonar and Radar

Sonar is a means of detecting the direction and distance of an object by reflected sound waves. The word "sonar" comes from SOund NAvigation Ranging. Sonar is used to locate submarines or other underwater objects. It uses sound waves transmitted through water to find them. When a sonar transmitter sends out sound waves, the waves bounce back after hitting a target. The sonar receiver then measures time and direction and can determine the exact location of a target. But it cannot be used to determine the location of a ship on the surface.

During the first years of the war, U-boats liked to attack while on the surface and after dark. They could not be detected by sonar and, because of darkness, they could not be seen. Then radar (RAdio Detection And Ranging) was developed. This system uses radio waves through the air in the same manner that sonar uses sound waves through water. Radar and sonar were both installed on convoy escort vessels. The ships could thus detect enemy submarines both on the surface and underwater.

Huff-Duff to the Rescue

Using High-Frequency Direction Finding equipment (HFDF — called "huff-duff"), ships at sea could intercept enemy radio transmissions. HFDF was used both on the shore and on ships at sea. When two stations tuned in on radio transmissions from the same target, they could determine its location. When a U-boat was located in this manner, speedy destroyers would steam to the area to attack the enemy.

High-frequency radio-telephone also was improved rapidly as the war progressed. Voice communication between ships and aircraft became possible. Even when completely hidden from view at night or in heavy fog, ships and aircraft could communicate with each other.

HFDF also allowed Allied radio operators to intercept German radio traffic. U-boats needed to be in regular contact with their commanders on land as well as with other ships in a wolf pack. The Allies used decoded German radio messages, huff-duff, and finally radar and sonar with great success. British and U.S. convoy escorts began to locate and defeat the wolf packs.

The Hedgehog

The crews of escort vessels became skilled in the use of sonar and huff-duff. But they often lost contact with a U-boat as they dropped depth charges around it. Depth charges are large, barrel-shaped explosives that can be preset to explode at a given depth. The explosions of the depth charges interfered with sonar reception. A new type of weapon was needed.

The "hedgehog" was the answer. It was a strange-looking weapon that was able to fire at one time 24 small bombs similar to depth charges over a submarine that had been located by sonar. The hedgehog missiles would sink into the water and explode only if they made a direct hit on a U-boat. So, if hedgehog missiles missed, there was no explosion and the sonar could still track the target. If a hedgehog missile did hit a target, it meant the end of a submarine.

An Aerial Umbrella over the Atlantic

Early in the Battle of the Atlantic, the RAF Coastal Command and aircraft flying from Canada could provide little air cover for convoys. The convoys had no protection from the air for most of their voyage across the Atlantic.

New, long-range aircraft became available, however. And by 1942 almost total air cover across the Atlantic became a reality. Merchant ships were converted into small aircraft carriers and sailed with the convoys. They could carry about 12 fighters or torpedo bombers.

U.S. Navy escort carriers and accompaning destroyers provided protection for convoys in the Atlantic.

An American Liberator bomber used by the RAF on anti-submarine patrol in the Atlantic Ocean

Finally, giant Sunderland flying boats, the American-made Liberator bomber and Catalina PBY flying boats became available. Taking off from bases in the British Isles, Canada and Iceland, they were able to patrol the Atlantic from shore to shore. They were able to provide almost constant air cover for convoys at sea. Just sighting a patrolling bomber would force a surfaced U-boat to stop an attack and dive for cover.

The Atlantic Ocean had been a great hunting ground for German U-boats from 1939 to 1942. Thousands of ships had been sunk, valuable cargoes were lost and brave men had died. But U-boat losses had also been heavy. With fewer than 100 U-boats at sea at one time, losses of five or six U-boats in just one convoy attack were too great. At last, in 1942 Admiral Doenitz, commander of the U-boat fleet, stopped Atlantic convoy attacks. He turned his attention to the shipping lanes along the Eastern seaboard and Gulf Coast of the United States.

Chapter 8

U-BOATS OFF NEW YORK

Following the Japanese attack on Pearl Harbor, the United States declared war on both Japan and Germany. Hitler and his U-boat fleet commander, Admiral Doenitz, ordered submarines to proceed to the East Coast of the United States.

The U.S. Navy was caught completely by surprise. Most escort vessels were busy guarding convoys. No one seemed to know how to defend against this new menace. In the month of January 1942 alone, 14 ships were sunk. And the U.S. Army Air Corps was of little help. Flying antiquated O-47 observation planes and B-18 bombers, the air corps conducted search patrols. They found nothing. Merchant ships traveling alone, not in convoys, were easy targets for the attacking U-boats. By the end of May almost 100 merchant ships had been sunk in U.S. coastal waters.

U-boats Hunt by Night

With the United States now at war, all coastal cities were supposed to be blacked out at night. But few people paid any attention to the rules. Bright city lights silhouetted the merchant ships passing a few miles out at sea. This made merchant ships excellent targets for U-boats. To avoid detection by aerial and sea patrols during daylight hours, the U-boats would rest quietly several hundred feet below the surface. Night became their time to hunt.

Finally the navy got smart and organized a system of convoys. By the summer of 1942 both the navy and air corps were better trained and had the ships and planes to protect the convoys. From bases in the Caribbean all the way to

As German U-boats swarmed into U.S. waters, dozens of merchant ships were sunk along the Atlantic coast.

Canada, small convoys with air and sea escorts would sail by day. At night they would put into a harbor. This foiled the nighttime U-boat attacks.

But submarines were still active. As coastal U-boat defenses in the Atlantic improved, Doenitz shifted his attention to the Gulf of Mexico. There the U-boats enjoyed a minor "blitz" when they sank 41 ships during May 1942. This activity also extended south into the Caribbean and threatened the Panama Canal.

The U-boat campaign in American waters was a great success. By July 1942 over 200 merchant ships had been sunk in western Atlantic approaches to the United States and in the Caribbean. At least 12 U-boats were active at all times off the U.S. Atlantic coast.

The U.S. Navy had been completely unprepared for coastal submarine defense. It took many months before the navy could stop the marauding U-boats. The science of anti-submarine warfare was just taking shape. If the war was to be won, the German fleet of U-boats had to be contained and then destroyed.

Chapter 9

ANTI-SUBMARINE WARFARE — VICTORY AT SEA

At the close of 1942 and into the early months of 1943, Admiral Doenitz's U-boat wolf packs went back to the Atlantic to attack convoys. But the convoys had become larger and faster. The Liberty Ships and other new merchant ships were swift. Surface escort vessels, now manned by sailors skilled in the use of their new weapons, screened each convoy day and night. They succeeded in destroying attacking U-boats at an ever-increasing rate.

And almost constant air cover gave the convoys greater security. The patrolling bombers attacked surfaced subs with deadly accuracy. But Hitler and his high command urged the U-boat fleet to keep fighting if Germany was to win the war.

Doenitz Withdraws U-boats from Atlantic

In March 1943 the U-boats scored heavily for the last time. Attacking wolf packs in the North Atlantic sank over one hundred Allied merchant ships. But from that time on everything changed. Bad weather interfered and convoy defense worked almost perfectly. When Admiral Doenitz counted up the score, he found that about three U-boats were being lost for every two Allied ships sunk.

The Capture of the U-505

The fortunes of war were turning against Germany in late 1943 and spring 1944. The U-boat wolf packs had been

American Captain D. V. Gallery in the conning tower of the German U-505 after its capture

defeated. The desert war in North Africa was won. And D-day — the date the invasion of France was to begin — was almost there. Only a few U-boats now roamed the Atlantic.

On June 4, 1944, just two days before D-day, an American task force under the command of Captain D. V. Gallery was on patrol in the South Atlantic. Suddenly a submarine contact was made. The USS *Chatelain* dropped depth charges with great accuracy. Its target, the U-505, severely damaged, surged to the surface.

Immediately the deck guns of the *Chatelain* opened fire on the wounded U-boat. Two fighter aircraft from Captain Gallery's flagship, the escort aircraft carrier *Guadalcanal*, strafed the doomed submarine. The German crew abandoned their sinking ship helter-skelter. They expected it to go to the bottom within minutes. But the abandoned U-boat stayed afloat.

Under command of a young navy officer, Lieutenant Albert David, a boarding party reached the U-505. Ignoring the fact that the sub might blow up or sink at any minute, Lieutenant David jumped onto the conning tower and dropped inside the German sub. Salvaging the ship's papers, he sealed off damaged sections of the sub and kept it afloat. He was awarded the Congressional Medal of Honor for this act of extreme bravery.

The *Guadalcanal* then placed a prize crew aboard the U-boat, attached a steel cable and began to tow the captured sub back to a U.S. base in the Caribbean. The U-505 was the first enemy vessel to be captured on the high seas since the war of 1812. The U-505 can now be seen on exhibit at the Museum of Science and Industry in Chicago, Captain Gallery's hometown.

U-boats Defeated by Force of Numbers

It is estimated that on any one day during the summer of 1943 the Allies had 1,350 merchant ships at sea. They were accompanied by hundreds of escort vessels. More ships were coming from U.S. shipyards daily to replace any losses. On the other hand, there were fewer than a hundred U-boats at sea at any one time. These were scattered throughout the Atlantic and in European waters.

As President Roosevelt had proclaimed before the war, the United States had become the "arsenal of democracy." The industrial might of the United States had provided the ships and the weapons that defeated the U-boat threat.

Victory at Sea

U-boats continued to be active on a lesser scale until the end of the war. But by the summer of 1943, they were no longer a major threat to the Allies. Hitler's submarines had been defeated by the combined might of Great Britain's Royal Navy and the Atlantic fleet of the U.S. Navy.

By the end of the war over 4,500 merchant ships had been sunk. Germany had lost 785 U-boats. For every Allied ship lost, two more took its place. The Germans' once-mighty U-boat fleet had shrunk to less than 200. The lifeline of convoys to Europe was made safe from attack. A great victory had been won. The Battle of the Atlantic was over!

U.S. scout bombers watched over convoys as they sailed across the Atlantic.

A Closer Look at . . .

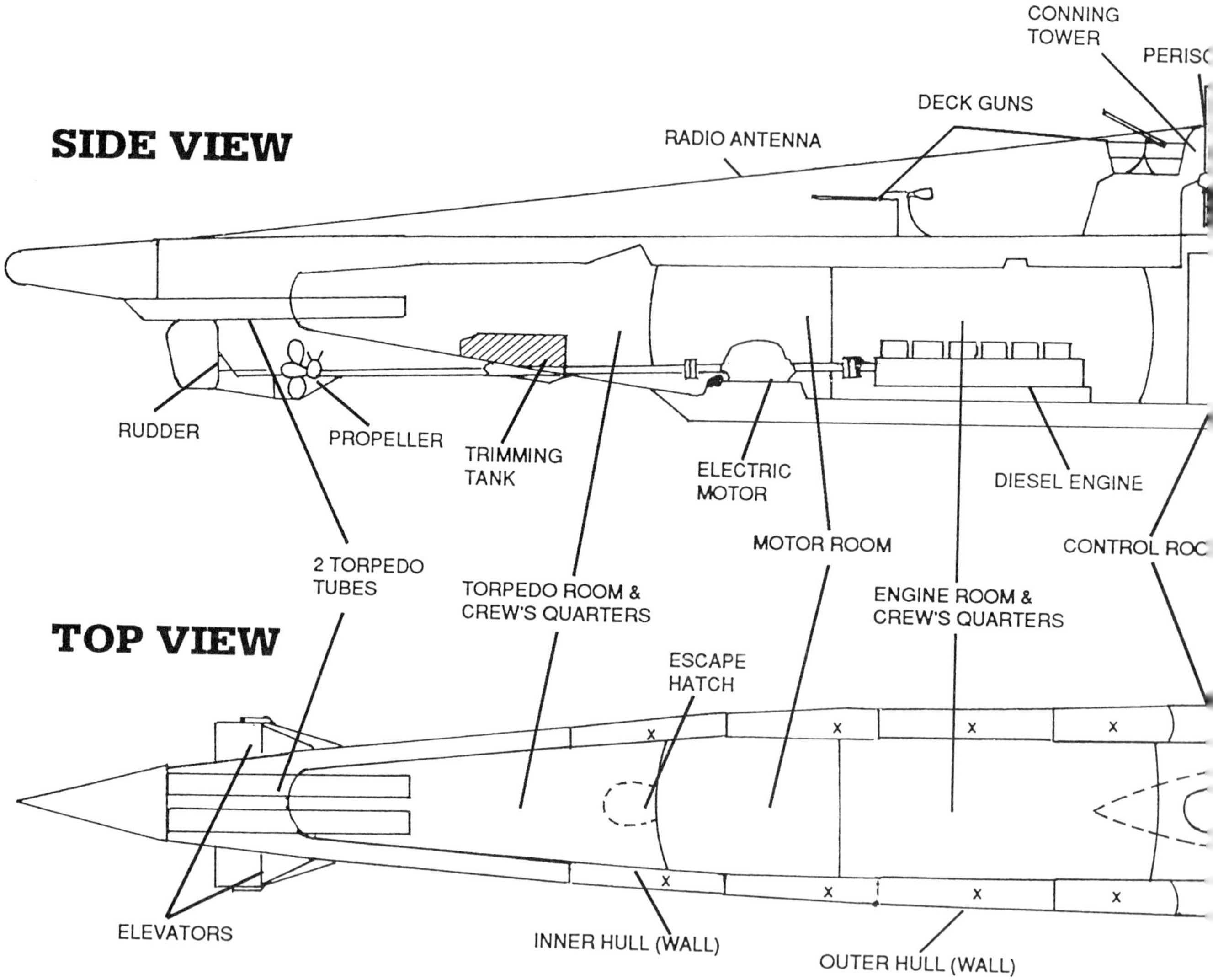

Tonnage - 1,200 tons
Length - 235-245 feet
Crew - 4 officers and 56 enlisted men
Speed - surface - 18 knots (about 20.7 miles per hour)
submerged - 8 knots (about 9.2 miles per hour)
Torpedo tubes - six
Torpedoes carried - 16-18
Range - surface -14,000 miles, submerged - 95 miles

Surface Operation — When cruising on the surface with the conning tower and other hatches open to outside air, a submarine operates like any other surface vessel. It uses regular diesel engines to drive a propeller.

A GERMAN U-BOAT

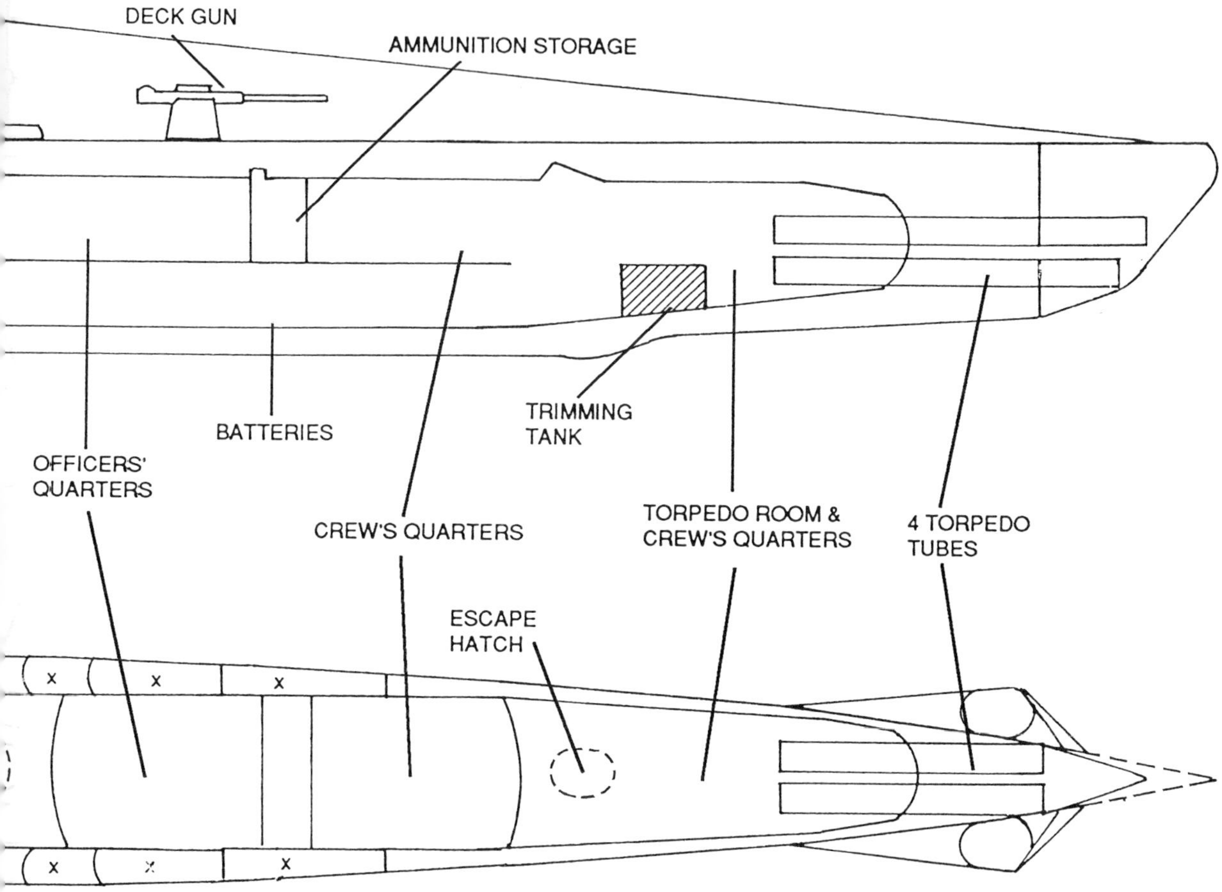

X = FUEL, AIR & WATER STORAGE

Submerged Operation — With all hatches sealed a submarine can cruise underwater. Oxygen and compressed air are used for ventilation and breathing. Large storage batteries are used to provide electricity to run motors to drive the propeller. Fuel tanks are built into the double walls of the U-boat. Other tanks in the walls are used for compressed air and water that help keep the ship level and to assist in maneuvering the ship to various depths.

A Closer Look at . . .

GERMAN U-BOATS

Inside a U-boat. Life on any submarine is difficult at best. Space is so limited that sleeping quarters can be located anywhere, even in the engine room. Limited supplies of everything from food to air make undersea life for submariners difficult as well as hazardous duty.

A Badly Damaged U-boat. With decks awash, this sub has been abandoned by its crew and is about to sink.

ALLIED SHIPS AND PLANES

Giant Battleships — HMS *Duke of York* (*left*)was the most powerful ship afloat at the start of World War II. As the war progressed, battleships fell prey to both enemy submarines and aircraft.

Escort Carriers Played a Major Role — Converted from a merchant ship, this early carrier (*right*) helped defeat the U-boat wolf packs.

Destroyers, Greyhounds of the Sea (*left*) — Fast and highly maneuverable, U.S. and British destroyers were armed with deck guns, torpedoes and depth charges as they protected Atlantic convoys.

Sunderland II Flying Boats (*right*) patrolled the Atlantic in search of U-boats with great success.

GLOSSARY

aircraft carrier A flat-topped ship on which aircraft take off and land.

Allies The nations that opposed Germany during World War II: Great Britain, the United States, the Soviet Union and France.

anti-aircraft Large cannon or machine guns used to shoot at attacking aircraft.

battleship The largest modern warship.

Catalina PBY A twin-engine amphibious flying boat used for long-range anti-submarine and scouting patrols.

conning tower A raised and semi-enclosed structure on the deck of a submarine used for surface control and as an entrance and exit.

convoy A group of merchant ships sailing together with navy escorts for protection.

corvette A small destroyer.

cruiser A high-speed warship, next in size to a battleship.

depth charge A barrel-shaped explosive set to explode at a specific depth, dropped from ships or aircraft on submerged submarines.

destroyer A small naval vessel used to escort other ships.

Kriegsmarine The German navy.

Luftwaffe The German air force before and during World War II.

merchant ship A civilian ship that carries cargo and passengers.

mine An underwater or underground explosive.

minesweeper A ship equipped to locate and destroy mines at sea.

pocket battleship A German warship ship slightly smaller than a battleship.

radar Radio equipment that detects airplanes and ships and determines their distance, speed and altitude. Short for RAdio Detection And Ranging.

sonar A system using transmitted and reflected sound waves to locate objects underwater. Short for SOund NAvigation Ranging.

subchaser A small, high-speed naval vessel used to track down and attack submarines.

submarine A naval vessel armed with deck guns and torpedoes which can operate on the surface or underwater.

torpedo A self-propelled underwater missile that explodes on contact with a target.

torpedo plane Aircraft equipped to carry and launch torpedoes.

U-boat German submarine; short for *Unterseeboot*, or undersea boat.

INDEX

6
7/11